The Christmas Promise

From Eden to the Magi

Jerry M. Henry

CROSSBOOKS

CrossBooks™
A Division of LifeWay
1663 Liberty Drive
Bloomington, IN 47403
www.crossbooks.com
Phone: 1-866-879-0502

© 2013 Jerry M. Henry. All rights reserved.

No part of this book may be reproduced, stored in a retrieval system, or transmitted by any means without the written permission of the author.

First published by CrossBooks 2/27/2013

ISBN: 978-1-4627-2365-2 (hc)
ISBN: 978-1-4627-2366-9 (e)
ISBN: 978-1-4627-2367-6 (sc)

Library of Congress Control Number: 2012922875

Printed in the United States of America

This book is printed on acid-free paper.

Any people depicted in stock imagery provided by Thinkstock are models, and such images are being used for illustrative purposes only.

Certain stock imagery © Thinkstock.

Scripture taken from the King James Version of the Bible.

Scripture taken from the Holman Christian Standard Bible ®
Copyright © 2003, 2002, 2000, 1999 by Holman Bible Publishers. All rights reserved.

Because of the dynamic nature of the Internet, any web addresses or links contained in this book may have changed since publication and may no longer be valid. The views expressed in this work are solely those of the author and do not necessarily reflect the views of the publisher, and the publisher hereby disclaims any responsibility for them.

I dedicate this book to the special gift God gave to me – my wife, Susan. She is my encourager and my supporter. It is not good for Jerry Henry to be alone, he needs Susan! We magnify the Lord together. (Psalm 34:3)

Introduction

The Christmas season has been labeled in song as the most wonderful time of the year. The decorations and the music reflect a holiday atmosphere that is so exciting. Christmas stories abound with fantastic characters who do all kinds of imaginary things that contribute to the spirit of the season.

There is one story, however, that is grounded in history and carries the opportunity of eternal impact—the biblical Christmas story. It began in the garden, where humankind sinned against the Creator, and the one who was wronged made the promise to set things right. He had an amazing solution that could only come from the heart of God. What began as a promise in the garden found fulfillment in the manger. The journey of that promise never loses its appeal.

This book is about that story. The first chapter opens with the problem of sin and death. Disobedience brought judgment, but it also carried the promise of the Redeemer. The hope for that Redeemer sustained God's program throughout the Old Testament.

Chapter 2 gives a portrait of the Redeemer as painted by the prophet Isaiah. The Spirit guided the prophet to write about one who would be despised and rejected. The markings of weakness and failure would characterize the substitute bearer of humankind's sin. This humbleness would begin with a simple birth.

The third chapter begins the Redeemer's birth story as found in the New Testament. John the Baptist was the forerunner for Christ's ministry. John's birth connected with Jesus' birth, but his birth involved an old priest and his wife. They were past the age of bearing children, but their miracle baby set in motion the promise made in the garden.

Mary's commitment comes out in chapter 4. She became the mother of the Christ child through a faith response to God's call. Her involvement has all the mystery of the virgin birth—a mystery only God could accomplish.

Joseph was also a major player in the Christmas story. Chapter 5 details this man's struggle and obedience concerning Mary and the Christ child. There was more involved than the carpenter understood, but his trust in God's directions showed a faith that displayed acts of courage. Chapters 6 and 7 tell how angels gave shepherds and wise men invitations to visit the Christ child. Both came out of darkness. One came from nearby while the others came from far away. Both needed special revelation, and both had to move from where they were to where the child was located. There was humbleness in both groups. With the wise men, there was violence from the established king. Despite the king's hostility, the promise found fulfillment.

All of this is fascinating to the mind and inspires the heart. While there is so much about Jesus' birth, the entire panorama helps to introduce the Savior. Introducing Christ through the biblical stories has a joy that is the true spirit of Christmas.

This story has brought me so much amazement. It caught my attention as a child. My first PhD seminar on this topic increased my interest, and my years of ministry have only added to its intrigue.

My desire is that the reader will feel the pulse of God's love as He brings His solution to our spiritual darkness. In the Christmas story, we find with the psalmist that "the Lord is good, His mercy is everlasting, and His truth endures to all generations" (Ps. 100:6, KJV).

Chapter 1

Christmas Promised in the Garden

Christmas! What comes to mind when you hear that word? Is it brightly wrapped gifts under the tree? Is it children so excited they can't sleep as they wait for Christmas morning? Is it a manger? When did it all begin, and what is it all about?

Christmas started long before the manger in Bethlehem. In fact, it started in the garden in the context of Adam and Eve's judgment. God made a promise that He eventually fulfilled. God proved to be a promise maker in the garden and a promise keeper on that first Christmas morning.

Unlike the Christmas classic "Rudolph the Red-Nosed Reindeer," the story of baby Jesus really happened. Rudolph was an imaginary character that went from zero to hero. The other reindeer laughed at him, but he ended up going down in history when he guided Santa's sleigh.

Rudolph may continue to entertain, but the fulfillment of the God-promised Savior goes beyond entertainment. It is God's offer of salvation that gives the hope of eternal life. Seeing the context of sin in the garden gives us appreciation for the fulfillment of grace at Bethlehem.

Genesis painted the creation scene. God spoke the world into existence. There was nothing but the Godhead—God the Father, God the Son, and God the Holy Spirit—and then there was something. It was a created world that was not only good but also very good (Gen. 1:31). Emptiness and void became cosmic order, full of life and beauty. The big things were there, like the darkness and light, but the small things were also there, like the stars that added sparkle.

Everything was in place, put there by the power of the spoken word of God. The Master Builder brought His A-game to the creation project, and His signature radiated throughout the created world. Even now, after the fall, all of us look at a sunset in admiration of a job well done.

Into this scene, God constructed a garden where He planned to put His crown of creation—humankind. He made the man first and gave him the task of keeping the garden and naming the animals. As he completed this latter task, Adam recognized his need for companionship. Something in his life was missing, and God moved to fulfill that need in an amazing way. God fashioned Eve from Adam's rib and brought her to the man. This "wow" moment in the garden was the first wedding—a moment that produced the first love song. The occasion seemed to require it. Weddings that the Lord orchestrates still inspire music from the heart.

God also gave the couple guidance. To create all that was created and then to withdraw would have been cruel. As sinless as Adam and Eve were at this moment, they were not all knowing. Their instructions were simple: they were not to eat from the Tree of the Knowledge of Good and Evil (Gen. 2:17). Their obedience to God's command was a choice that kept them from death. Paradise was such a secure place—a place where man and woman could express their best and enjoy a safe environment.

Although Adam and Eve followed God's rule and His imprint was everywhere, there was still the need for God's personal presence. To meet that need, God came to the first couple in the cool of the day (Gen. 3:8). It was a God-initiated appointment that happened on a regular basis. The inspiration of personal time spent with the Creator no doubt filled the depletion that living in even the garden of Eden brought. Although sin was absent, the humans needed to be refilled with God's presence on a regular basis. These moments of worship spent in fellowship with God were so necessary. Their souls were restored with the life-sustaining energy of the creator God. Their humanness hungered for the power only the presence of God could fulfill.

Why change this? Everything seemed to be going so well. Disruption didn't come from listening to God's voice but to another voice in the garden. The evil one's approach was so subtle and nonthreatening. His conversation took Eve's attention away from God's word and put it on the forbidden fruit. The more Eve listened, the more she moved toward doing what God had told her not to do. She ate of the fruit and gave to her husband. They both ate what they knew they shouldn't eat (Gen. 3:6). Listening to the evil one had a destructive price tag; it always does!

The inner shame came. It flooded the cores of their beings. Outward eating had inward action. The guilty couple was driven to cover themselves—totally disregarding their care for each other. Hiding things now became more important than being open.

Adam and Eve hiding from God at their meeting place did not keep God from them. God came to them and worked to draw out confession—"Where are you?" (Gen. 3:9). The question was meant to surface a rebellious attitude. It was not a request for information.

Heaven's greatest work was now set in motion to repair the brokenness of humankind's sinful condition. God did what He had to do; He punished the wrong and enforced justice. For God to ignore their disobedience would have been worse than the wrong itself.

First God cursed the serpent with an existence of conflict. He would creep and crawl in dirty places and exchange blows with Eve's offspring. The evil one would create so much dysfunction, but the fatal blow would come from Eve's child (Gen. 3:15). Here is the first promise of Christmas. It says so much about God's character that He put His personal hope in the middle of judgment.

God also passed out other judgments. No one escaped from the results of wrongdoing. Eve would deal with pain and sorrows that were multiplied in her offspring. Life now had a painful end as well as a painful beginning. The solution to the sinful condition was bringing forth life out of pain. No doubt, the shadow of the cross hung over this moment.

Adam had to deal with the sorrow and frustration

that would characterize even his best efforts. As a man formed from dust, he would battle the elements of life, only to fall victim to its demands. An uphill struggle would keep dogging man's steps until he returned to dust (Gen. 3:17–19).

Where do we find Christmas in this mess? Certainly the Grinch had his victory. There were no Christmas carols in this moment. The crowded malls would never open if the story had ended at this point. Gloom, despair, and misery are the only songs to flow from this situation. If it were not for God's grace, then life would be hopelessly unbearable.

In the midst of this judgment and gloom, there was a glow of grace. It was not full blown. So many pieces of the puzzle were needed to fit the picture back together. However, there were elements that would take the birth, death, resurrection, and return of Christ to complete the full picture.

Three gracious gifts gave the Genesis situation hope. These came from the very heart of God and represented the Lord's commitment to the salvation of humankind.

He refused to give up on the crown of His creation. The Lord not only created, but He also recreates. What had been sold into the slavery of sin by the first Adam He would set free through the work of the second Adam—Jesus Christ (Rom. 5:12ff).

The first grace gift was the promise of a deliverer. The exchange of blows between Satan and Eve's offspring would take place in the context of history. The entire Old Testament and New Testament would paint a clearer picture. Enough was said in this garden moment to assure the couple being judged that evil would not have the final word. A baby that Mary delivered and placed in a feeding trough would be the fulfillment of the promised one. For so many years the people of God would live with this hope of the coming one. What God promised, He delivered.

The second grace gift was the animal covering. God installed a system for dealing with sin on a limited basis. Behind the action was the sacrificial death of an innocent animal. Innocent blood was shed to cover the sinful couple. Animal sacrifices provided a holy God's basis to provide forgiveness. Full payment came from the once-for-all payment on the cross (Heb. 9–10). The spiritual genius of the Creator was on full display as He applied His love to the sin problem and delivered His own solution. It makes for amazing reading. It also causes the sinner to raise his/her hands to thank God for the gift of salvation—a gift that no one deserves. The Lamb of God does take away the sin of the world (John 1:29).

The third grace gift involved the guarded access to the Tree of Life. Evil did not close the door to eternal life, nor can humankind come without accepting God's plan. The access is a guarded access. The cherubim with the flaming sword ensure that the way to God can come only by God's way (Gen. 3:24).

Sinful humankind would have an existence without hope if he lived forever in sin. Death in this way is both a judgment and a hope. Life with death is a much better alternative than a sinful life without ending. The stark reality of death should cause a person to look for the offer of eternal life—and God has provided that way. In fact, it is the only way (John 14:6).

Adam and Eve were cast out of the garden. They moved out of their secure world into a very scary world. It is no wonder that the most frequent command in Scripture deals with fear. Because of sin, fear is life's constant companion. So much insecurity exists when one is distanced from the source of security. Death stalks the living, and regrets and misunderstanding become a way of life in even the best of human relationships. Humankind's sinful condition made it harder and harder for them to hear God's voice. The God who at one time had been so near now seemed so far away.

However, God's plan is in place. Evil will not have the final say. The couple lost its glory but has the hope of a glory to be regained. Adam and Eve had the promise of the Redeemer, the provision of sacrifice, and the guarantee of guarded access to the Father.

Christmas is a long way off. God's plan of salvation is amazing, but it comes in sequence. Noah must see a rainbow; Abraham must start a nation; Moses must receive the Law; David must lead his nation; and a couple must move from Nazareth to Bethlehem. God had given humankind a forward look with a promised Savior and had set in motion all that was necessary to make the first Christmas happen.

Adam came out of hiding, received his animal covering, and made the first faith statement in the Bible (Gen. 3:20). In the face of the death sentence, he grabbed hold of the sure hope that God is the life-giver. His heart impression had a faith expression. Christmas would be a mother-child situation that would bring God's redemptive solution.

As Adam and Eve left paradise, they carried their hope and trust in the God who created them, who would sustain them, and who would move heaven and earth to redeem them.

Chapter 2

Christmas Promised in Isaiah

As we continue along on our journey of Christmas, let us look in on a little boy and his dad who were shopping for a Christmas puppy. Each puppy was so cute, but one was more noticeable by the way he kept wagging his tail. That puppy captured the little boy's attention, and he said, "Dad, I want the one with the happy ending."

The little boy recognized his Christmas present. Isaiah's prophecy concerning the Servant Messiah helps us recognize our Christmas present too. That present was more than a baby in a manger; it was the Savior who died on the cross.

Through the lenses of the prophet Isaiah, we are given a perspective of the kind of Savior Jesus would be. If we listen to Isaiah 52:13 through Isaiah 53:12 with our hearts, we will feel the pain of the sacrificial lamb. We need to see for ourselves the death of Jesus for our sins so we can rejoice in the good news of God's forgiveness. This allows Isaiah's picture to give us the right Christmas perspective but also to help us see the joy of God's happy ending.

Isaiah stands tall among the prophets. He spoke God's truth to four different kings and through four generations of Judean Hebrews. His written word brought godly inspiration to so many situations. Like Abel, his ability to speak went far beyond his death. His book is called a "vision" (Isa. 1:1), and his inspired insights influenced New Testament writers more than any other prophet did. Some highlights include the shaping of John the Baptist's ministry (Mark 1:2ff), the direction of Jesus' ministry (Mark 1:11), the context of Jesus' first sermon (Luke 4:18ff), and Paul's missionary strategy (Rom. 15:21). With Isaiah's blueprint of the

Servant Messiah, the Christmas story is more than a fable of a man in a red suit. Instead it starts the exciting drama of the baby in a manger becoming the Savior at the cross.

The first half of Isaiah deals with the judgment of God's people who have given themselves to idolatry (Isa. 1–39). The second half, however, focuses on the hope after judgment. Significant in this hope are the descriptions of the coming servant. Bible interpreters label these as the Servant Songs. The final song (Isa. 52:13—53:12) outlines a suffering and glorification that gives life to those who believe. It is the crown jewel of Old Testament writing because it portrays the vivid details of substitutionary atonement.

Isaiah lived in the eighth century BC but prophesied about what Jewish exiles would face in the sixth century BC. Throughout the Servant Song, the verbs are past tense, but the prophet saw them as happening in the future. This prophetic certainty described the actions as fulfilled long before they actually took place.

Let me encourage you to take a deep breath. Put on

your eyes of faith, and follow a pre-Christmas description of the Savior. It will not be a warm, fuzzy story, and at times, it will have the horror of a brutal slaying. However, the admonition of Isaiah from beginning to end is to keep our eyes on the servant—"See my Servant" (Isa 52:13 HCSB)—and experience the wonder of the Father at work. A strength-in-weakness program would not be man's solution, but it is God's solution—and nothing can be better than God's solution.

Isaiah 52:13–15 is the first of five stanzas that contain three verses each that show wisdom as defined by God. Such wisdom is not based on outward appearance, for it has the look of failure, but from the outset, the end result is a matter of not only glory but also very high glory (v. 13).

Although the servant's appearance has the marks of extreme mistreatment, the impact will carry a cleansing that has global implications. Power figures will be speechless at God's provision for sin. Theirs would be a first hearing with amazing results. Paul's reading of this passage inspired him to adopt a missionary plan of carrying the gospel to those who had never heard. (Rom. 15:21)

The second stanza (Isa. 53:1–3) begins with two rhetorical questions that anticipate negative answers. They voice the hard sell of the Servant's message. He is not a crowd pleaser but represents God's powerful presence. Those who understand Him as God's redemptive plan will do so not from popular speculation but only by the Holy Spirit's revelation.

For the servant, His boyhood would be under God's direction, but the conditions included humble surroundings as well as a struggle for survival environment. Neither His origin nor His appearance creates popular appeal. The Hebrew nation was on the lookout for the Messiah, but no second looks came Jesus' way. He was too ordinary. Furthermore, a carpenter's son from Nazareth did not fit the profile of a national deliverer. However, God can come in the least likely people and in the least likely places. Can anything good come out of Nazareth? With God the answer is always yes!

Isaiah 53:3 is not a pleasant read. Isaiah spoke of the

servant as despised—a word used twice for emotional emphasis. Like Esau who despised his birthright (Gen. 25:34), the crowd would act in complete refusal toward the servant. The despised one would also be the rejected one. These two forms of stinging opposition would be the response directed toward this man of suffering. Such association with suffering caused people to write him off as a failure. People turned away from Jesus in total rejection. A suffering Messiah was not the answer they wanted. Even Jesus' closest disciples found this picture hard to swallow (Mark 8:32).

Isaiah's message was that the servant would relieve suffering by suffering. It will take the resurrection to understand the crucifixion. Rigid religious expectations often are the enemy of seeing some of God's most powerful moments. Christ's identification with sinful humanity means He understands our hurts, but that identification would take him to the cross.

The servant profile fulfilled at the cross seems less entertaining than a sleigh with eight tiny reindeer. God, however, continues to use the story of the cross to open the door of many hearts. What appears so foolish to some is the power of God to those who are being saved. Such is the wisdom of God (1 Cor. 1:18ff). It will take the eyes of faith to see this as God at His best because a surface look wrongly categorizes Christ as weakness and failure.

Isaiah 53:4 begins the transformation process. Watching the servant has a payoff. We begin to see the despised and rejected one for who He really is. Instead of casting accusations, we are forced to look at the iniquity He carries for each of us.

Now we begin to see. Blamers dramatically become confessors. Here is the power surge of innocent suffering changing the hardest of hearts. Pronouns dominate this section, making a defining moment that each must experience for himself/herself.

The servant's uphill climb has the weighted burden of disease-infested humanity. It is a misunderstood event initially, but eventually it is seen as God sanctioned. The misread is that the servant is out of God's will while, in fact, He is in the very center of God's will.

Then right perspective suddenly dawns on the viewers. The guilty ones see their guilt being shouldered by the innocent one. Healing happens when the servant absorbs our guilty blows. God's peace only comes through the wounded healer. Since all have sinned, all are in need of this Savior (Rom. 3:23).

Being compared to straying sheep is not a compliment. If it were not for the shepherd, the sheep would be hopeless and helpless. God's solution is not to abandon the herd but to move toward humankind with the lamb of sacrifice. Jesus not only felt the pain of the sinner, but He also paid the price for the sinful. What is made available for all must be received by each one. All who are forgiven stand at the foot of the cross and shout at the top of their voices, "Jesus paid it all." Only forgiven sinners can sing this song with the heartfelt emotion it deserves.

Silent suffering characterizes the suffering death of the servant. The fourth stanza (Isa. 53:7–9) carries this point. Twice the reader is made aware of no response to obvious abuse and hard mistreatment. No one has had a greater right to retaliate, but He never did. One expects to hear words that loudly express the intensity of one facing the tragedy of such extreme injustice. However, the quietness of the sufferer communicates volumes. Such silence comes from meaning beyond the moment. It is being in control while all else is so out of control. The absence of ballistic fireworks shouts of a depth of purpose that refuses to be shaken.

Isaiah compares the Suffering Servant to a lamb being led to slaughter (Isa. 53:7). The picture given is that of a silent walk to death. The meek animal makes no appeal on its way to the killing place. Insult is added to injury as the legal system places a convicted criminal's death sentence on the innocent servant.

Death comes—not an ordinary death but one made horrible by painful means. In fact, the scene painted is that of hard blows of the worst sort. The deathblow meant for sinful humankind falls on God's provided substitute. The display of character in the face of mistreatment is attention grabbing; the servant never threatens his executioners.

Evil seems to have claimed another victim. The added insult was being buried with the wicked. Indignity added to indignity heaps shame on a sad ending. However, even the burial was a place where secret disciples became bold witnesses (John 19:38–42). Never underestimate the power of God to use even the worst situations to show forth His glory.

The character of the Suffering Servant in these verses has such a magnetic draw. A repentant thief confessed his own guilt and reached out for salvation (Luke 23:39–43). A hardened executioner felt the need to shout out that the servant was God's Son (Mark 15:39).

When treated meanly, the servant did not become mean. When given the worst form of abuse, He never backed away from His purpose. This patient endurance has been the example for Christian martyrs through the ages. Their standing fast in difficult circumstances focused on the one who stood fast in His difficult circumstance. Suffering in this context can become one's finest hour (1 Peter 2:21). It shouts of an inner source of strength that only those in the middle of God's will can know.

The final stanza (53:10–12) lets us know that there will be more to this story. It gives clues that the crucifixion and resurrection will fulfill in detail later. An amazing transformation has taken place in this song. Those who begin pointing at the servant as guilty have recognized their own guilt. This recognition of the substitutionary sacrifice is the only remedy for humankind's sin.

Isaiah strongly emphasized that the sacrificial death had a planned purpose. God's approval as well as His directing activity surfaced repeatedly. A problem existed with humanity's sin and God's holiness, so God initiated reconciliation through the substitute death of His Son. An unstoppable redemption has been achieved, and it is waiting for the repentant sinner to receive it.

The Servant rescues many as His reward of faithful obedience (Isa. 53:12). The death of one brought the divine benefit for many. His sacrifice is sufficient for salvation. Divine justice is satisfied. Believers step into God's presence because the righteous Servant paid for their iniquities. God conquered evil His way.

Luke records the story of the Ethiopian's conversion (Acts 9:26–40). Philip was pulled from a revival in Samaria and sent to a desert road. As a chariot came by, Philip heard an impressive stranger reading Isaiah 53:7–8. Philip then led the Ethiopian to understand this passage as fulfilled by Jesus. What was needed was for the stranger to receive the Savior's sacrifice as payment for sins. He did, and Philip baptized him as a sign of the Ethiopian's faith. This is not a Christmas story, but it is a salvation story—one made possible because the Savior came at Christmas.

All of us, like the Ethiopian, need to allow Isaiah to lead us in worship and acceptance of the servant's sacrifice. When we receive Jesus' sin-conquering death, we also receive His life-giving resurrection. Here is the greatest gift ever given to humanity—the Savior of Christmas. Hallelujah! What a Savior!

Chapter 3

The Forerunner's Birth

In 1970, while serving in Vietnam as a first lieutenant, I was able to get an R & R at Christmastime. My wife flew to Bangkok, Thailand, to meet me. We were ready to celebrate Christmas in a place where Christ was not celebrated. On Christmas Eve, we were blessed to find an English-speaking church that had a service focused on Christ. Our hearts were hungry to enjoy the fellowship of other Christians and again enjoy the story of the Savior's birth. The service was one of those never-to-be-forgotten moments that affected our lives.

Luke's version of the Christmas story begins with a

never-to-be-forgotten moment—the birth of John the Baptist. John was a major player in the life of Jesus and was the last Old Testament prophet and the first Christian preacher. His role as the preparer for the entrance of Jesus required a special birth. It was told through the lives of his parents—Zechariah and Elizabeth.

This couple's story tugs at the heartstrings. Even though they were too old to have children, the childless couple had a child. Zechariah lost his ability to speak but recovered his voice and sang to a surprised audience. The audience pondered what had happened and smiled in approval at the wonder of the events. This is too much to be ordinary; the supernatural was happening. The Messiah was on His way, but first we must hear John's story to get us ready for Christmas.

As we face a world that is so distracted at Christmas, may John's birth bring our attention to Christ. In a culture so obsessed with consumption, we need to open our hearts to the biblical story of God becoming man.

The first Christmas happened within the context of

what appears as God-forsakenness—an idea predicted by Isaiah. A prophet for God had not spoken in Israel for four hundred years. However, in the midst of spiritual dryness, an old priest and his wife remained faithful.

Zechariah was a priest in the division of Abijah—one of the twenty-four priestly divisions that served in the temple complex. His wife, Elizabeth, was also a person of strong faith. They both put their hearts into their walks with God and demonstrated their trust, even when life appeared unfair.

The couple's heart's desire was to have a child. Having children would bring the joys of parenthood but would also be a contribution to the future. The pain of being childless was compounded by the talk on the street that labeled Elizabeth as "the barren one" (Luke 1:35). Maybe neighbors entertained thoughts that God had withheld children from Zechariah and Elizabeth because of sin in their lives. All of us tend to fall into the trap of wrongly assuming why God does what He does.

The couple prayed, but their situation seemed

unchanged. The dream of having a child faded with the years. A sinking reality of childlessness as a permanent condition took hold. However, the story had not ended. What is impossible with man is always possible with God. He is never overwhelmed by the size of our problem. Zechariah and Elizabeth challenge others to faithfulness by maintaining godly lifestyles in spite of disappointments or unfulfilled dreams.

One cannot read the situation of Zechariah and Elizabeth without recognizing the echo of Abraham and Sarah. Both were couples who had a child when they were physically unable. What God did before, He can still do now. He still delights in taking empty situations and filling them with His solutions.

Circumstances for the saintly couple took a decided change when Zechariah was chosen for service in the temple. An Old Testament way of discerning God's will was to choose by lot. Zechariah was chosen, and it was an opportunity of a lifetime for the old priest. The privilege of officiating at the incense burning in the holy place was the height of a priest's ministry. Only a few got to serve. For Zechariah, his standing alone in the holy place became a God-filled moment.

All of a sudden an angel was standing to the right of the altar. This was not listed on the temple bulletin. Luke did not describe the angel's appearance, but we learn that his name was Gabriel. Angels were active in the birth stories and the empty tomb events. In fact, God created angels to worship and serve from God's immediate presence.

Zechariah's response to Gabriel's appearance was one of great fear—not just fright but off-the-charts fear (Luke 1:12). Anytime the supernatural confronts humankind, the first response is one of great fear. The picture painted is that of a very frightened priest not knowing what to say or what to do.

Gabriel broke the silence and spoke to the moment. His words are the first direct quote in Luke and were given to calm the priest's fear. The command of "stop being afraid" is the most frequent command in Scripture. A fear mindset could be the greatest hindrance to an exciting adventure God has planned for us.

That the angel spoke the priest's name had to be significant. That the God of the universe knew an average priest's name should have brought some form of reassurance. Gabriel further reassured Zechariah of his answered prayer. These reassuring words may mean that Zechariah took the opportunity to pray for his nation and also to include a personal prayer for a son. My understanding is that God had answered his prayer when it was offered years before, but He was waiting for the right time to bring the answer to reality. God's silence for the long years did not mean His absence. The moment had finally come on God's timetable to deliver the answer. His timing is not always our timing, but His timing is always on time.

Gabriel's words were words the priest had dreamed of hearing: his wife would have a son (Luke 1:13). God's new way of working with humankind through Jesus Christ was about to dawn. Promises made long ago were starting to be fulfilled. God would use this faithful couple to reach others by giving them a son who would turn people to the Lord (Luke 1:16–17). Their son would be blessed by God throughout his life and ministry as the Messiah forerunner. Even the Holy Spirit would guide and strengthen him to accomplish God's purpose for his life. All Zechariah had to do was to receive the message by faith and name the child John.

One must stop at this point and acknowledge how Zechariah and Elizabeth had been faithful even in difficult circumstances. They had to wait on God when He seemed to be so distant and silent. They stand with so many who have been in their place only to survive through prayer. Their example was to follow even if God's answer is no. God will provide strength to make it through. Paul found that grace, and it was sufficient (2 Cor. 12:9ff).

When Gabriel finished his announcement to Zechariah, one would think the old priest would have shouted for joy. That didn't happen. Doubt crept in his mind, and the priest focused more on his disability than God's ability. From his doubt and fear, he asked for a sign to give him the certainty that his doubting demanded (Luke 1:18).

Zechariah's attitude of expectation had taken several hits. His hope had perhaps risen with earlier prayer meetings, only to be dashed with the frustration of another disappointment. After so many hurts, the wound of disappointment runs deep and a person crosses the line of despair. An inner wall is raised to guard against further disappointment, but it takes a toll on godly expectations. His fear of another disappointment cried out for the certainty of a sign.

Gabriel, on the other hand, identified himself. His words to the priest came from the very presence of God. That should have been enough. However, he did give the priest his requested sign: he would be unable to speak (Luke 1:18). The old priest then went out to bless the people in a public ceremony, but because of his speechless condition, he could only make motions. Those who were perceptive saw something in the speechless priest that indicated he had experienced God. However, he was unable to communicate his exciting news. That had to be a major frustration.

Somehow Zechariah communicated the good news

to Elizabeth. When he went back to his Judean hill ministry, she became pregnant. What the angel had told him was being set in motion, and even God's most dedicated servants stood in amazement. We should never underestimate the power of God or become too rigid in our expectations. A pregnant Elizabeth hid herself and her condition but had the smile of blessing that those who have found God to be faithful have.

The circumcision ceremony was ingrained in the Hebrew tradition. Its origin went back to Abraham and the sign of being set apart for God (Gen. 17:9–14). The community gathered when the baby boy was born to Elizabeth and Zechariah for the circumcision ceremony (Luke 1:59). The event was a celebration with food and singing that climaxed with the naming of the child. The party atmosphere was a celebration to thank God for this new life. In fact, the lives of Zechariah and Elizabeth had come full force from the time of stagnation, when God seemed so distant, to a time of celebration, when God seemed so near.

So much had taken place since the Zechariah-

Gabriel meeting. Elizabeth had become pregnant, Mary had become pregnant with Jesus, and the two expectant mothers had met. Their meeting was a Holy Spirit encounter—a sure sign of God's presence in the events taking place. The two women were experiencing more than they understood but were assured of being in the center of God's will (Luke 1:39–56). God's new initiative included both their sons, and the excitement was more than they could bear. With the circumcision of the baby boy, the synagogue celebration was now ready for the naming of the child. What had been a private experience at the altar of the temple was now ready for public expression. Everyone assumed the baby would carry his father's name. In their defense, it was the customary thing to do.

However, those present had not heard Gabriel's message. Elizabeth stopped the naming process and adamantly stated that the baby's name would be John (Luke 1:60). The relatives resisted with an argument as old as time itself: "We have always done it this way." Elizabeth refused to give in to the crowd's pressure and stood up to the opposition. Their wrong insistence was met by her right insistence.

The relatives appealed to Zechariah. They did not want to give up on their old ways. The old priest, now a new father, was suddenly the center of attention. His answer would reflect his faith. Had the months of enforced silence brought about the needed change in attitude? Once he was called upon, Zechariah motioned for a tablet. He wrote four words that broke the chain of unbelief: "His name is John" (Luke 1:63 HCSB).

This act of faith brought a "wow" from the audience of relatives. Things were happening that were beyond their ability to grasp. Certainly the environment of anticipation was raised to a new level when Zechariah recovered his voice and broke out in a loud song. What had been frozen by an act of unbelief was now opened by an act of faith. The naming party had future expectation written all over it. God was up to something, and the excitement it generated spread throughout the community. Acts of obedience are so contagious.

Zechariah could not let this moment pass without a

song. Perhaps it was more than a song; maybe it would be better to call it a sermon in song (Luke 1:67–79). The sermon Zechariah was unable to give at the temple gathering he now gave with much force at the naming gathering. His temple audience waited and was disappointed, but his audience at the naming heard a message that had the inspiration of restored, godly expectation.

Academics calls Zechariah's song "the Benedictus," from the Latin translation of "blessed." Prophecy had been silent for four hundred years, and this represents the prophetic voice that had been waiting a long time to be heard. It is significant that God is blessed because of what He is doing, and what He is doing goes back to promises made to Abraham and to David.

This was Zechariah's final contribution to the Christmas story. He delivered his prophetic song and then disappeared from the biblical stage. The story went on, but the old priest faded into the background. Despite an earlier setback, he allowed God to use him to set the stage for the long-awaited Messiah. He gave up on God in the past, but God did not give up on him. Redeeming people is God's trademark.

To all of us who have blown opportunities at the worship altar or have failed to speak when the audience was ready and waiting, the example of Zechariah gives us hope. God still does wonders with first-chance servants, and this is so affirming. He also does wonders with second- and third-chance servants. He can fix failures.

Zechariah's song was Spirit-inspired and Spirit-delivered. He thanked God for the Savior that was coming. All the anticipation of the Old Testament would find fulfillment in the events that were about to happen.

The old priest then addressed his son (Luke 1:76ff). John would follow the blueprint outlined by God. His ministry would spotlight the work of Jesus. His preaching set in motion a sense of expectancy that created the atmosphere of readiness to receive what only Jesus could deliver.

John preached the forgiveness of sins to a people

who considered themselves sinless. His messages were in-your-face confrontational to turn those whose hearts had grown hard. The shock of this would point out the tragedy of sin and the rescue available in the one coming. John knew that he was not the solution but was being used by God to point to the one who was the solution.

Zechariah emphasized that God's work in Christ would be a "dayspring visit" to those in the darkness of despair (Luke 1:78–79). Hopeless pilgrims in the grip of sin and death would be able to see the light of hope with the ministry of Zechariah's son. There was divine purpose written into the child's life at an early age.

God assigned the most important message of his day to John. As John introduced Jesus to his generation, so must we introduce Him to ours. Nothing in the world compares with sharing the gospel with someone and seeing God use us to bring the message of eternal life to a lost person. May we be as faithful as John was with our assignment. Perhaps God will use our witness to prepare others to receive the Savior—the Savior of Christmas.

Chapter 4

Mary's Commitment at Christmas

Christmas happened because God made a commitment to humankind at the garden. It also happened because a peasant girl in Nazareth committed her life to God's plan that the angel offered her nine months before Christmas. She became a major player in the Christmas story as the mother of the Christ child. Her commitment story remains a must read that continues to inspire hearts to have a "Mary Christmas."

Mary had the experience of being chosen by God. This experience is not always comfortable and often drives the chosen person to his/her knees. The decision Mary made was costly at times, but the payback came in impacting a world for the gospel. Her commitment to God's offer became an occasion for heavenly rejoicing outside Bethlehem as well as the generations that have followed her example.

God initiated a sequence of events that connected John's birth with Jesus' birth. The sixth month of Elizabeth's pregnancy became the trigger point for Gabriel being sent to Nazareth. These two births were pivotal parts of the salvation blueprint God was working to save humankind.

Gabriel had appeared to Zechariah in the temple at Jerusalem, but now he came to Mary in Nazareth—a place of least expectation. God is unlimited in the places where He may approach us. For Moses, it was in a desert place; for Isaiah, it was in the temple; for Paul, it was on a road to Damascus; for John, it was on the island of Patmos. To be too narrow in our expectations of where God can and may speak may cause us to miss His work.

Luke identified Mary in three descriptions. First she was a virgin, meaning a young maiden without a sexual experience. Mary was most likely in her early teens, and her virgin status was necessary for Jesus as both human and divine. Jesus was born of a virgin not to make Him the Son of God but because He is God's Son. His conception was like no other. The great God above us would become the God with us in the most fragile and smallest of human forms—a baby. A special conception was necessary for this special baby. Divinity was packaged in humanity. Jesus was both divine and human.

Mary was identified as engaged to Joseph. She had gone through a commitment ceremony that brought about a binding status between Joseph and herself. They were waiting out their year of engagement that would be finalized in the Jewish wedding ceremony. Such was the social custom of their world.

Joseph had a pedigree. It was essential that he was of the house of David. This connected Jesus by adoption to the promise made to King David of a forever kingdom from David's family (2 Sam. 7:12–13). Jesus would be the ultimate fulfillment of that promise. Time never erased God's promise nor does it erase the kingdom Jesus established. Without Jesus, there is no forever kingdom.

Finally Luke identified the young maiden by name—Mary. She was a person of worth and dignity who became a model of discipleship. Certainly she is to be admired but not worshipped. As a woman, Mary made a decided contribution in a society that neglected the potential of so many women.

It is frightening to realize that Mary could have said no to the angel. Like the rich, young ruler, she could have walked away from the Lord's offer and would have never been heard from again. So much hung in the balance waiting for the agreement of a teenage girl.

Gabriel had a direct approach. He walked into her moment with a greeting that instantly got Mary's attention. In a rapid-fire greeting, Gabriel extended an invitation to rejoice, told of her chosen status, and assured her of God's presence (Luke 1:28). The greeting came packaged with joy, grace, and power. This hello had God's approval and made a statement.

In fact, the greeting shocked her. She was deeply troubled by the words as well as the one who spoke the words. Like a computer in search mode, Mary's mind sorted through the situation. Connecting the dots was not easy. It is a tribute to Mary's courage that she stood her ground while making sense of the matter. Mary could have run away.

Gabriel continued to seize the initiative. His words were designed to bring calmness to a troubled heart—"stop being afraid" (v. 30). What the angel was about to offer staggered the imagination, but it came straight from God. Of all women, Mary was the object of God's favor—His choice. To be favored by God is to receive an assignment in His redemptive program. Such assignments can only be accomplished with a Lord-with-you strength. This is the crucial factor, for without God, we can accomplish nothing of lasting significance (John 15:5)

Mary continued to listen. Her already-stirred

emotions seemed to remain calm as Gabriel mapped out God's plan. First, she would conceive; second, she would give birth to a Son; and third, she would call His name Jesus. All three actions triggered so many questions. Her mission was indeed a mission impossible.

The name Jesus means "the Lord saves." It is a heaven-given name as well as a common name. This one who carried that name would be defined by the God who gave the name He carried. He was God's saving purpose. Mary's maternity would affect eternity, for Jesus would establish the eternal kingdom of God.

As with Mary, God calls us to opportunities of service only He can accomplish. His call may come wrapped in confusion and fear, but it has the opportunity of heart-pounding joy. One of the worst tragedies is to live this life and miss being fully alive spiritually because we refuse a favored role that God offers us. Choosing to follow God's will for your life has a high cost of involvement, but choosing not to follow God's will has an even higher cost of noninvolvement.

Knowing God's purpose and submitting to that

purpose are two different matters. The first does not guarantee the second. Mary was at that crossroads of decision where she could either say yes or no—submit or reject.

The angel spelled out God's offer for Mary to give birth to the Savior. When Zechariah was told of John's birth, he asked for a sign. Mary, on the other hand, asked a question. A questioning faith is not out of God's will.

Becoming a mother was a farfetched idea to an engaged virgin. She needed more information. Mary's straightforward question was strengthened as she re-emphasized her lack of sexual experience. Biologically, her ability to conceive was out of the question, and Mary pointed this out with her statement of virginity. To Mary's credit, it was a fair question that needed a good answer.

Gabriel did not frown at Mary's question. Hers was not a lack-of-faith question but a quest for information; heaven invites those kinds of questions. Sincere questions delight God's heart.

The kind of defensive response Gabriel demonstrated toward Zechariah was absent in his response to Mary. Using parallel actions, Gabriel described the activity of the Holy Spirit in Jesus' conception. It would be a "come upon" action similar to the Pentecost filling of the Spirit (Acts 1:8). There also would be an "overshadow" movement like the cloud at the scene of the transfiguration (Luke 9:34). God's Spirit would creatively work to conceive a baby in Mary's womb without sexual activity. Such power was of the Most High that produced the holy child and the Son of God. Mary asked the question; Gabriel gave her the answer.

Gabriel felt Mary's struggle. Processing all this had to be difficult. She needed something more. Therefore, the angel added a sign to build his case. Mary's cousin Elizabeth was in the sixth month of a pregnancy that humanly speaking couldn't happen, but it did. A struggling Mary needed the kind of assurance that Elizabeth's pregnancy would give her. Mary didn't ask for a sign, but one was given to strengthen her faith.

All of us need the inspiration of what God is doing in someone else's life.

Gabriel further added a Scripture verse. Reaching back into Israel's history, he brought forth a verse that described Sarah's pregnancy (Gen. 18:14). God delighted in making the impossible possible then, and He still makes the impossible possible now. God is still in the business of accomplishing the impossible. Mary now had an answer, a sign, and a verse of Scripture, but would she trust and submit?

What would Mary do with what she now knew? The ball was in her court. Hers was a life-changing decision, but more than that it would affect so many other than herself.

Mary's answer of yes was forthright. She expressed complete submission and used the slave term to describe herself. A slave was one sold out to another. This was not reluctant surrender but a ready faith that agreed wholeheartedly with whatever God was about to accomplish.

At the end of this scene, Gabriel left. His leaving had

to be more than a walk out. I picture him returning to heaven with the flair of mission accomplished. There had to be heavenly celebration with glorified shouts of praise. Mary's yes brought salvation to the world. It causes me to shout because Mary's yes brought salvation to me—praise the Lord!

Submitting to God's purpose is such a defining moment. We never know the impact of that decision on ourselves as well as others. May Mary's yes to God's purpose guide us in saying yes to God's purpose in our lives. Let us acknowledge that when we surrender to obey and serve the Lord, He transforms us and uses us in His saving work.

After Mary signed on as the Lord's bondservant, she immediately went to see Elizabeth in the hill country (1:39). The meeting of the two expectant mothers carried a double blessing. Elizabeth's baby leaped within her at Mary's greeting, and a Holy Spirit–inspired moment followed. The old and young were coming together under the supernatural work of God. Their time together was a source of great strength for both women. All of us need what another Christian can bring to strengthen our Christian walk.

Mary's response to all that had happened was a song. She could not keep her feelings inside. They exploded in words labeled as "the Magnificat" because she magnifies the Lord in the song. In fact, her song came from the depths of her innermost being—her soul and spirit (Luke 1:46–47). Drawing from the spectrum of the Old Testament, Mary interpreted her experience through Scripture. Here was a mind that had thought through and reflected upon the experience of others. Mary especially drew from Hannah's song (1 Sam. 2:1–10). Scripture acted as her guide in processing her perspective.

A much-needed aspect of the Christian life is to feel our faith. Mary's song provides an example of faith being expressed in feelings. Her song burst forth from her heart. The overflow of her heart reached for words from Scripture to express her intense feelings. Mary was an obedient servant, giving full expression to the God who acted in history and was now acting in her history.

The note of joy resounds throughout the song.

Gladness came because the God who was Savior in the past is also Savior in the present. Hers was not just a Savior moment but a "My Savior" moment; the pronoun makes the difference (Luke 1:47). What God has done for others, He had now done for her.

Mary's social status as a peasant girl was a humble condition that did not disqualify her for service in God's kingdom. That God looked with favor to include her filled the young maid's heart with astonishment. This shock of inclusion gained momentum in praise as Mary looked to blessings for future generations. Her attitude was not prideful but a humble thankfulness that could not get over what God had done and would even continue to do.

Themes from Mary's song would find fulfillment in the life of Christ. The empty would be filled, the humble would be exalted, and the exalted would be fed. Acts of mercy would amaze those acted upon. It is significant that Mary finished her song with the word *forever*. God's mercy reached out to the dark world and gave what only God could give—a forever.

The Christmas Promise

The evidence of a life touched and changed by God is a thankful heart. Mary stood amazed that the God of the past had worked on her behalf in the present and would continue to work with future generations. Her thankful heart had to sing. The push of gladness refused to be suppressed. She became the first to sing a Christmas carol.

What amazing changes has God done in your life? His gracious work toward each of us should inspire a joyful song. For Christians, Christmas carols are more than mouthing words but are so personal. They become expressions of thankfulness for the God who can be counted on to take the impossible and make it possible—for the God who not only makes promises but also keeps His promises. Herein is the hope that Christmas brings.

Chapter 5

Joseph's Commitment at Christmas

Joseph's role in the Christmas story had a different kind of commitment. He had to listen from the perspective of a hurting fiancé and decide to take on the marriage of Mary and the baby. Everything surrounding Mary's pregnancy was beyond the comprehension of the village carpenter. His part was not a speaker's part, for he is not directly quoted in Scripture even one time. However, his obedience to God's direction saved both Mary and the Christ child. Of all the fathers in Scripture, Joseph stands the tallest. God handpicked this earthly father for the assignment that was so world changing. He rose to the challenge of his Christmas decision with the steadiness of a man who hears God's voice and obeys it—without question.

Matthew focused on Joseph in his version of the Christmas story. The Hebrew audience to whom he first wrote would have been impressed with Joseph's ancestral link to King David. As the story unfolds, Joseph's character shows itself in acts of principle and compassion. His righteous behavior reflects a humble dependence on God's guidance. One has to admire this simple carpenter.

Before Matthew told Joseph's story, he set up the genealogy of Jesus. It shows how organized Matthew was because he listed three groups of fourteen names. The list traced the history of the Hebrew nation from Abraham to King David, from Solomon to the Babylonian exile, and after the Babylonian exile to the birth of Christ. Not everybody in the family line was listed, but the flow of history included both good reputations and bad reputations. What is established is that Jesus climaxed Hebrew history as both the Son of David and the Son of Abraham.

Noteworthy is the naming of five women in the genealogy. Scholars have scratched their heads trying to find a common theme. What seems to surface is that they were considered "shady ladies" in the scandalous things they did. Tamar (v. 3), Rahab (v. 5), Ruth (v. 5), Bathsheba (v. 6), and Mary (v. 16) all had to deal with a certain amount of scandal. These women kept alive the ongoing life of God's people through surprise actions. What God was doing through Mary must be counted as surprise action. A too-rigid expectation errs in writing God out of moments that He brings together. There is no such thing as a God-forsaken situation.

Jesus' birth had a scandal also. Mary and Joseph had committed themselves in an engagement ceremony and were waiting their year for the marriage ceremony. Hebrew custom considered them legally married, but the maiden remained with her parents for a year. No doubt the village of Nazareth saw the wedding as a social event already on the calendar.

Then Joseph found out that Mary was pregnant. Scripture gave a head's up that her condition was not from unfaithfulness but from the creative power of the Holy Spirit—a fact that Joseph found out later. As far as Joseph knew, Mary's pregnancy had an explanation that could only come from misbehavior. He appeared to be wronged by the very person he loved so much. This would be a severe test of Joseph's godly character. Joseph handled it well. He wanted to do the right thing—an action that would have God's stamp of approval. Paul will use this very term to describe the righteousness of God. In the face of seemingly wrongful treatment, Joseph extended kindness. He refused to let anger define the moment. He considered making Mary a public example but decided instead to divorce her quietly. On the surface, this situation had all the markings of an adulterous affair that would end in a separation—a scene all too familiar in our generation. The private divorce ceremony would take the place of their proposed public wedding ceremony. This situation did not appear to have a happy ending.

The planned divorce hit a snag, however, when God intervened. Joseph had a night of restless sleep. He couldn't let go of Mary. Writing her off, even if she had committed adultery, was not easy. Such an action did not fit her godly lifestyle. Besides, even if she had done wrong, he still loved her. The feelings would not die.

Somewhere in this restless sleep, the angel of the Lord entered through the process of a dream. Joseph would have four angel appearances in dreams, and each would give God's direction for him to follow.

The angel spoke to Joseph's heart. His first matter of consideration was to stop being afraid to marry Mary (Matt. 1:20). Fear could have kept him from the best thing that ever happened to him. A second consideration was that the baby was a product not of unfaithfulness but of the Holy Spirit. Mary's pregnancy was not of sin; it was a God thing. The breath of heaven produced the baby in Mary's womb. The third consideration was to name the baby Jesus—a name that would identify Jesus' mission. He would save His people from their sins. That was the fourth consideration; His mission was a rescue mission.

Wow! What a dream. It became a life-changer for

Joseph. Matthew felt compelled to give more insight on the condition of Mary. He used his usual method of reaching back to the Greek version of the Hebrew Bible for confirmation. For Matthew, the birth of Jesus was an anticipated event. Five hundred years earlier, Isaiah spoke of a God presence so real in the birth of a child that it would be a God-with-us situation. This Immanuel factor framed Matthew's gospel, for it appeared at the beginning (Matt. 1:23) and at the end (Matt. 28:20). This promise of presence was also there as the church gathered in Jesus' name; He is present (Matt. 18:20).

The mystery of a distant God came near in the birth of Jesus. Divinity became flesh in the form of a little baby. For Matthew, the virgin conception with the nearness of God needed extra reader attention, so he placed a "behold" in front of the Scripture affirmation. He used it to punctuate the angel's message (v. 20), and now he uses it to accentuate the meaning of Jesus' birth. It is Matthew's way of saying, "Don't miss this!"

When Joseph woke up, he changed his mind. The

decision he had made before to divorce Mary quietly was reversed. A planned divorce was avoided because of the insight that came from God's messenger. God brought Mary and Joseph back together.

Joseph's obedience was immediate and with complete dedication. That full obedience to the angel's direction came through his commitment to Mary and the child she carried. It was probably a private ceremony, but the impact would be worldwide. When the baby was born, Joseph stepped up and named the Christ child the name he had been directed to name him: "he called his name Jesus" (Matt. 1:25 KJV). Mary was a virgin fiancée, a virgin bride, and a virgin mother. The birth of Jesus was a total creative act of God the Father, God the Son, and God the Holy Spirit. The Trinity was fully employed at Christmas.

Joseph's father role did not end with the birth of Jesus. Though not the biological father of Jesus, this carpenter rose to the occasion of taking care of his little family. The angel spoke to him in a second dream (Matt. 2:13). God spoke to Joseph with a sense of urgency and in the dream, told him to get up immediately. He was to flee to Egypt, for Herod's soldiers were on their way to kill the child—go and go now!

The instruction and explanation brought Joseph's rushed response. He got his family up and out on the road to Egypt. Never mind that nighttime travel had so much danger in desert routes. The danger of staying had more threat than the danger of going. Besides, the carpenter had a trust in God that would send him and his family into the night.

Herod's soldiers came to Bethlehem. They killed innocent baby boys two years old and younger. Death and pain entered the Christmas story as children were being slaughtered by an insecure ruler. The world can be a dangerous place, even for babies. The Bethlehem massacre had all the plots of the Exodus story. At that time, God delivered baby Moses out of Pharaoh's hands; so now He also delivered Jesus out of Herod's hands.

Joseph took his family to Egypt. He was to stay there until he received further word. However, Egypt was not the place for Jesus to stay. He needed to return to Israel.

That was God's plan. The Exodus similarity with the nation of Israel comes out again in the life of Jesus. The old Exodus story was fascinating, but the new Exodus story (with Jesus) is even more exciting.

When Herod died, the land of Israel seemed to be a safe place for the Christ child. Joseph again received a dream revelation (Matt. 2:19–20). He was told to leave Egypt and return to the place he had fled. He set out for Bethlehem to raise his family.

The night flight, however, had left a lasting impact on the traveling father. As he and his family drew close to the nation of Israel, he heard that Herod's son was the new ruler. Archelaus' reputation was too much like his father. Joseph was afraid to expose his family to that kind of threat. His caution was verified by the revelation angel, and he changed his destination to Nazareth. Fear is not always a bad thing. Perhaps here was an early hint that Judea would be a dangerous place for Jesus. Joseph again made a good decision under God's guiding hand.

Nazareth was such an out-of-the-way place for Jesus

to be raised. It didn't seem to have much promise. The prophets agreed that this kind of place would be the growing place of the Messiah (Matt. 2:23). God's promises have a way of being fulfilled in unlikely places. Such is the wonder of the God who fulfills His promises in ways that cause us to stand in amazement.

Joseph's fatherhood shines so brightly. The baby he delivered was the one who would deliver the world from sin and death. His decisions of obedience demonstrated a trust in God that was rewarded. He remains a walking definition of true manhood.

Joseph may never have been quoted, but his actions speak louder than words. A simple carpenter made an eternal mark because of his commitment. The impact of a godly father has so much potential. His example helps so many to make right decisions in the crossroads of life. Joseph's place in the Christmas story is that of a hero. What a man!

Chapter 6

Shepherds See Promise Fulfilled

A little girl was given a bubble-making machine for Christmas. It was a gift she was happy to receive, but it was unassembled. Her father put together the machine, and the little girl was eager to take it outside and fill the Christmas Day air with bubbles. The problem, however, was that the manufacturer recommended Joy as the detergent of choice to use in the machine, and they were out of Joy.

The little girl's father gave her the bad news: "We don't have any Joy. The stores are closed, and we have to wait until tomorrow to buy Joy." What a letdown. They were all set up and ready to bubble, only to be disappointed because they were out of Joy. For too many, their Christmas will be spent without joy.

The first Christmas was an event full of joy. The angels announced to the shepherds that God had fulfilled His promise to bring His light of redemption to a world darkened by sin and death. A Savior had been born, and the shepherds would be the first to experience the joy of this heavenly deliverer. The biblical Christmas joy does not come from a store but from the gift of receiving the Savior.

The first Christmas had no Christmas trees, no presents, and no carolers at the manger scene. The barren surroundings of Mary, Joseph, and the baby seemed to cry out for a drummer boy. This challenging circumstance appeared as if God was absent. However, God was never more present. In fact, He is there in the darkness of a nighttime experience, even when you don't see Him or feel Him.

Luke is the only gospel writer who described the birth of the Christ child. The story was set in motion when Caesar Augustus, the Roman emperor, needed money to finance his campaigns. His solution was to have persons register for the purpose of being taxed, a taxation decree that was carried out in Roman provinces. Since Joseph was a law-abiding carpenter, he obeyed the rule of Rome. His attitude, along with his fellow Jews, must have been: "I'm doing this, but I don't like it." Registration for a tax, especially from an occupying enemy, is never a happy occasion.

Above the actions of this global leader—the world's most powerful ruler at the time—were the actions of Almighty God. He was bringing together His salvation plan that He had first made known in Genesis 3:15. God worked the decree of a pagan ruler to accomplish the fulfillment of the Old Testament promise. To the Jews, this taxation decree seemed like another harsh treatment at the hands of hated Roman authorities. Here was another bad thing that God turned to good. Augustus's decree became the catalyst to fulfill the prediction of Micah 5:2.

Joseph and Mary journeyed from Nazareth in

Galilee to Bethlehem in Judea. The journey of about one hundred miles had to be difficult for Mary. It was important because of God's promise made years earlier that David's heir would be born in Bethlehem.

The city itself had no reputation for rebellion. The rich grain-growing region gave the city its name; Bethlehem means "house of bread." Here David had herded his sheep and learned the valuable lessons from God as a shepherd. Songs that came from the future king's heart were stimulated in the fields outside Bethlehem. This special place to David would be the place of Jesus' birth. Luke interpreted the journey while Matthew cited Micah 5:2. As frustrating as this might have been to Joseph and Mary, it was a fulfillment to David. The God he had come to know in his childhood was still active in accomplishing life's events. He is and remains a God who handles promises with the utmost respect. You can count on Him.

Mary had reached the point of full term in her pregnancy. The couple's stay in Bethlehem would be short lived. The city itself was overrun with angry tax registers. Where Mary delivered the baby Jesus is still debated. It could have been a cave, or it could have been a place in the bottom floor of a house that was used to stable animals. Room was at a premium under such crowded conditions. What was made available became the place of the birth. Jesus was delivered under difficult circumstances in a place that was given. His mother wrapped the newborn—the Son of God—in the strips of cloth used by peasants and put him not in a bassinet but in an animal feeding trough. This was a far cry from heaven. Could this be the plan of God? It sure didn't look like it.

The word *joy* does not appear in the birth of Jesus (Luke 2:5). Luke writes this verse with the matter-of-fact approach of a professional. One would have thought he should have put more into the birth scene. The contribution of so many has been to bring a drummer boy, wild-eyed animals, and songs of excited carolers. They were not there. The scene of the Savior's coming into the world didn't have a drum roll—and neither did His departure. God sometimes comes in matter-of-fact circumstances, but the movement He sets in motion will be earth shattering.

The word for gospel means good news. In a world where there is so much bad news, the gospel delivers a good-news message. Sin and death need not be the last word. In fact, the love of God brings His solution to the glaring deficiency of humankind. God reached out in love to meet the deepest need of the human heart with the Savior who alone can meet that need.

The shepherds were the first to receive the gospel. They heard it in wonder and responded to it in faith. Theirs was a pattern of hearing and responding that would be followed by so many down through the ages. It is the way God gathers His people unto Himself. The very amazement of the gospel shatters the dullness of routine and turns shaking shepherds into singing shepherds. The good news is so spectacular that it comes with a "must tell" desire. The shepherds shared their experience and brought amazement from those who listened.

It is significant that Luke recorded more about the

effects of Jesus' birth than about the birth itself. The manger scene gets perspective from what happened to the shepherds. The change the good news brought to unsuspecting lives is an undeniable evidence of God's touch.

The shepherds were recipients of the initial Christmas invitation. Israel's family of origin included shepherds—Abraham, Isaac, and Jacob. Moses was a shepherd who had a burning bush experience. David was the hero king who took care of the sheep and was doing his shepherd's task when he was brought in from the fields to be anointed king. However, shepherds were also persons who were avoided rather than invited. God's invitation list must have been the only one that focused on shepherds. Remember, His list is the one that counts.

The shepherds were out in the fields, keeping watch over their flocks. No doubt the sheep were vulnerable to predators—both two-legged and four-legged. Night made their vulnerable situation more vulnerable. As watchful as they were, what happened next caught them completely off guard.

Surprise came to this nighttime scene. The darkness was suddenly illuminated by the appearance of an angel—not just any angel but an angel of the Lord. One moment there were the sights and sounds of the night, and then all of a sudden, the angel stood before them, with heavenly radiance all around them. In effect, God's messenger was bringing heavenly glory to the shepherds' earthly situation. Certainly God takes the initiative in pushing back the darkness—a move that brings hope to so many situations that are engulfed in the darkness of sin and death.

How did the surprised shepherds respond to such glory? They were terrified, and the fear that seized them was totally consuming. This is the third time that fear is the first reaction of those confronted with the plan of God—Zechariah, Mary, and the shepherds. The supernatural always overwhelms humanity's categories of comfort.

The angel's first words were directed toward this fear. It is a command repeated in Scripture more than any other command: "Don't be afraid." Here, as in the other infancy situations, the words of the angel were designed to bring calm to what appeared as a threat. The shepherds were not under attack but were recipients of the good news of salvation. Let the good news define the moment, not fear.

Now that the angel had the shepherds' attention, he preached the Christmas sermon. What the angel proclaimed to a wide-eyed audience was personal—a "to you" message.

Loaded into the personal message was the fact that it contained joy beyond measure—great joy. In fact, the listeners were not only the shepherds but would encompass all of Israel as well as the entire pagan world. The audience may change, but the message of good news with great joy calls for a personal response. What was personal then is personal now and can be received at this very moment.

The good news focused on the person of Jesus. In effect the good news told the shepherds who Jesus was and where they could find Him. The angel defined Jesus with three terms or titles: He is Savior—one who delivers the lost from their sinful condition; Jesus is the Messiah—the king and anointed one promised to Israel and David; and He is Lord—the one who rules and reigns and desires first place in our lives. All of these titles were in this one baby, and these simple shepherds were being addressed with the invitation to see this event for themselves.

Such a glorious event would certainly have glorious indicators. However, the described baby—Savior, Messiah, and Lord—was an ordinary child in appearance. The angel's guidance pointed to a baby wrapped in cloths and lying in an animal feeding trough (Luke 2:12).

These directions called for open-minded obedience. The baby of high character would be in low circumstance. An old person having a baby challenged Zechariah, a virgin conception challenged Mary, and a kingly baby lying in a feeding trough challenged the shepherds. Each challenge called for a faith response to carry out what God would do or had done.

Heaven, therefore, helped the shepherds see the

first Christmas for the splendor that it was. In fact, the entire heavenly choir showed up to give the Christ child the heavenly sendoff He deserved (Luke 2:13–14). Here was the sign given that emphasized the birth of the angel's message and directions.

The angelic chorus sang a song of reconciliation. The God in the highest had come to humankind on earth and offered peace to those who were graced with this offer. Although man had sinned against God, it was God who was taking the initiative to come to humankind. This is love not to the deserving but to the undeserving. In two balanced lines of song, the thousands of angels sang the Christmas carol to the watching shepherds who must have been amazed. The scene had to have been overwhelming.

All of this was an invitation to come. The angels disappeared, and the shepherds were left to respond to what had been seen and heard. Revelation that had come their way now called for a response. To experience the message and stay where they were would be to miss Christmas. It is still amazing how much we are exposed to but how little we respond. In a real sense, God had come to the shepherds, and now the shepherds had to go to the Christ child. They had to move from where they were and go to where Jesus was. The spectacular display of the angel of the Lord and the heavenly host would have been an empty experience if the surprised spectators failed to become sincere seekers.

As the angelic chorus faded and the night routine returned, the shepherds could not contain their excitement. Conversation was back and forth with the overflow that each felt. Their decision was unanimous: "Let's go" (v. 15).

Therefore, the shepherds hurried off. Theirs was the first Christmas rush. A literal translation of these words is, "They came hastening." With deliberate focus, they searched intently until they found the baby Jesus. The clues given were in Bethlehem, a baby newly born, wrapped in strips of cloth, and lying in a manger. No doubt they had to look in several places, but theirs was a determined search.

The shepherds found Jesus. Any life search without

the Christ find is an empty search. Mary and Joseph were also there. However, make no mistake, it was seeing the Christ child that ignited the shepherds' hearts. They became tellers of the story, and the rejoicing of the angels became the rejoicing of the shepherds. Seeing the Christ child had that kind of impact. Others needed to hear what the shepherds experienced. Mary and Joseph especially had a need for their encouraging word. Being in the center of God's will always thrives on the input of others who have received God's blessings.

The shepherds returned to their fields, but along the way, they shared with others the details of the night. The object of the shepherds' story was the child. All that happened dazzled them, but the focus of their message was the child (v. 17). The witness to others included the drama that drove the shepherds from the fields and flocks to the manger where the Christ child was found. Sidetrack issues faded in the telling, and the spotlight was placed on the child. He alone was the subject because He alone is God's salvation plan. The reaction of all who heard was one of surprise, for they were amazed.

Mary tried to piece together all of these happenings in her mind and make sense of what God was doing. She had experienced more than she understood. Her mind was so active in trying to pull all these events together. This added so much depth to her already deep faith commitment. Her heart had a baby book that held a treasure chest of God-filled memories. Those memories both stimulated Mary's mind and gladdened her spirit. Mary seemed to have the balanced blend of desire to understand and the thrill of a faith in touch with her feelings.

Christmas had finally come. So much had happened since the promise in the garden. Years of waiting had pointed to this moment. Of all the people groups, the shepherds were the first invited guests to experience the Savior. They set the pattern of a faith response that hears the message and comes to Jesus. The Christmas invitation still goes out and still ignites joy to those who receive God's gift in Jesus.

Joy to the world, the Lord has come!

Chapter 7

Wise Men Find Jesus

After Christmas has an atmosphere that can be described as busy. The anticipation of Christmas Day has come and gone, but the after-Christmas sales draw shoppers. Returning gifts that were too big, too small, or too over-the-top make the returning lines long. Getting back in the routine of life still has the holiday glow, but the enthusiasm is fading. New Year's offers some celebration, but for all practical purposes, another Christmas season has come to an end. Feelings that were so strong during the anticipation of Christmas are packed away along with the decorations and must wait until next Christmas to be inspired again.

Matthew has brought to us an after-Christmas Christmas story. His story of the magi who arrived from the East happens after the story of the shepherds. Those wise men were not at the birth of Jesus but showed up after He had become a child. However, their contribution to the Christmas story cannot be left out. Their journey to see the Christ child demonstrates the draw of Jesus from the far corners of the world. It is an after-Christmas story that has all the enthusiasm of Christmas day.

The wise men came a long way to worship Jesus. They fell to their knees before the Christ child and his mother because they knew the Savior was worthy of their adoration. Worshipping the Savior took first place in their lives. He was the object of their search, and when they found him, they went facedown with gifts worthy of one who would change the world one heart at a time.

Matthew's gospel tells us about the journey of these wise men. He records how these faraway Gentiles came and how they created a crisis of authority for the established king. These magi arrived unexpectedly; a special star had caught their attention and sent them on a search for the promised Messiah that it signaled. So much mystery surrounds both their origin and their designation, but their worship had worldwide significance.

The magi arrived in Jerusalem, the capital city of Israel and the primary palace of King Herod. Nobody in the city was looking for these visitors from the east, nor had anyone invited them. Their unannounced appearance caught the ruler off guard and left Jerusalem's inhabitants wondering what would happen next.

Who were these wise men? Scholars say these were men who studied the movement of the stars (astronomers) and applied that study to direction for life (astrologers). In other words, they sought heavenly signs to interpret earthly events. They seem to be a professional caste of philosophers, probably from Persia, who were both wealthy and powerful. Their influence in the Middle East was great, drawing the utmost respect from Herod.

A certain star had caught their attention. However, it did more than catch their attention; it kept their attention. A passion was ignited within their hearts that drove them to set aside their normal activities and go on a search that covered thousands of miles, endured hardships of the desert, and risked exposure to enemies. Their destination had an unclear start and was only satisfied when they fell at the feet of the Christ child. The worship experience was well worth the journey. The outsiders, coming from a great distance, found what the insiders were still looking for but were refusing to see.

The wise men's entrance into Jerusalem likely had an impressive impact on the onlookers. No doubt the caravan paraded into the city as a showcase of Middle Eastern affluence. It had to have been a dazzling sight that opened the eyes of the Jerusalem citizens who lined the streets. The scene certainly included more than three bath-robed men riding on three camels.

As impressive as the entrance was, it was the wise men's question that gained the most attention. They were seeking the location (where) of the newborn king who, they said, was born king of the Jews (Matt. 2:2). In fact, this question is the only direct question and statement recorded of the wise men. Location was asked and purpose was stated. They had come a great distance to worship this new sovereign.

Their question stabbed into Herod's heart like a dagger. He was the ruling monarch not by birth but by manipulation, assassination, and the approval of Rome. It is significant that these wise men kept asking the same question over and over—a continuous question that refused to be hushed.

The wise men's search had been triggered by a heavenly sign they said was His star (Matt. 2:2). Here was an eye-catching miracle of nature that appeared, disappeared, and appeared again. The heavenlies gave notice to those who were on the lookout that the Savior was born and a new age was dawning. The star signified the cosmic brilliance of God's love bringing light to the darkness of humankind's lostness. The wise men's journey was a journey of purpose to worship Him.

These rich foreigners were eventually brought to

Herod. Their question and purpose statement had reached the Judean king, and he felt deeply disturbed and threatened. His insecurities quickly surfaced. Therefore, before the wise men arrived, Herod wanted to appear in control with the right answer.

The king had a track record of power issues. In fact, Herod's intense insecurity kept bringing out his thug side, and even his own family became victims of murderous rampages to eliminate any and all throne claimers. His reputation as a killer was well known throughout the city, and any situations that aroused suspicions were taken out even on innocent persons. When Herod felt threatened, no one was safe, and as a result, all of Jerusalem was disturbed with him.

To provide the visitors with an answer to the whereabouts of this newborn king, Herod assembled the chief priests and scribes—the Hebrew Bible experts. The birthplace question came to these scholars more as a demand than information gathering, and the pressure was great to give the right answer. Herod was pressing them, and they knew it.

The experts were right on target with their answer. It is amazing how much they knew but how little they used the information they had. Their having the right answer was not translating in living the right solution. Such tragedy existed because they knew the Scriptures but were unable to hear the Word of God in their hearts. Knowing Scripture and even pointing others to Him is no substitute for finding Him yourself.

The religious scholars reached back to the prophet Micah for the prediction he had made through the inspiration of the Holy Spirit. Micah was an eighth-century BC prophet who gave assurance to wayward Israelites of a future restoration (from Assyrian and Babylonian captivity). He had long since passed from the scene, but his words were a living voice to each generation because of what was written. All of God's promises will be fulfilled.

Bethlehem of Judea was designated as the messianic birthplace (Matt. 2:5–6). It was a small village known for its grain growing. The community was not a hotbed for military action but a place of peaceful shepherds. What it did have was the connection to King David, a promise made and fulfilled by the promise-making God.

This little village was to be "by no means least"—a phrase that elevated the village to celebrity status. Other cities would pale in comparison to the future leader born in Bethlehem. His life would move untold numbers to submit to His authority. An insignificant beginning in a seemingly insignificant place would have global significance.

Jesus' leadership would have a shepherd character (Matt. 2:6). Such guidance would be of a pastoral nature rather than the fits of rage that characterized Herod. One was authority driven by compassionate care while the other was authority driven by self-centered insecurity.

Opposition came to Jesus from the beginning, even at His childhood. The Jewish leaders responded apathetically at the long-awaited Davidic king while Herod responded with hostility. Later, the Jewish leaders also would vehemently oppose Jesus. Such opposition would eventually nail Jesus to the cross. However,

God's plan in Jesus Christ was and is greater than any and all opposing forces. Those who stand against Christ are never able to stop Christ. He not only withstands opposition but also reaches out to save those who are against Him.

The biblical experts told Herod that the birthplace of the Christ child was in Bethlehem. Herod, therefore, knew where, but he did not know when. He craftily devised a plan to find out the age of the Christ child. Herod was so good at playing the role of backstabber.

Herod summoned the wise men secretly (Matt. 2:7). They seemed unaware of the king's evil plot and only detected later, by God's insight (v. 12), the king's true intent. This private meeting allowed the wicked king to question the magi without onlookers or curiosity seekers. He was making sure that such information would be for his ears only.

The king worked his web of destruction while maintaining the appearance of sincerity. It was the Grinch trying to steal Christmas. Put another way, it was the wolf in sheep's clothing. He masked his feelings and remained focused at the same time. This was no casual matter. In Herod's mind, his very throne was at stake. Herod had dealt with others and eliminated them, and this seemed to him to be another challenger to be put away. Instead of outright asking the age of the child, Herod focused on the exact time the star had appeared, which suggests the star was not now in view.

Having learned the time of the star's appearance, Herod sent the wise men to Bethlehem. He was going to use them as double agents. They would find Jesus and then inform Herod where He could be found. The king habitually used others to do his dirty work. It was a diplomatic maneuver. Herod was very clever.

Connecting the age of the Christ child with the appearance of the star may have been a clever disguise, but how accurate the timing was may be a question. The wise men could have seen the star and invested time in finding the answer through their own resources. Having exhausted their own sources, they could have finally set out on their journey. Regardless of their travel time, Herod now had a framework for the newborn king's age.

The wise men left their meeting with Herod unaware of his insincerity. He was so good at masking his badness. His parting admonition was for the wise men to search carefully for the child. Herod avoided calling the Christ child a king and said instead the child (Matt. 2:8). He couldn't force himself to say the word *king* even in hypocrisy.

Herod appealed to the wise men to report back with the location of the newborn child. I imagine at this point the wicked king paused to put his best look to his lie—"so that I can go and worship Him" (Matt. 2:8 HCSB). Herod was a worship pretender who used deceit to cover his true intention. The true motive of murder was hidden beneath the deceptive genuineness. What appeared so right was at the core so wrong!

The king convinced the wise men, and they bought his deception hook, line, and sinker. God saw what may have seemed sincere to the wise men for what it was; He was not fooled. Tragically, the very person Herod tried to destroy was his only hope for salvation. A different story could have occurred if Herod had submitted to

Jesus' superiority instead of opposing it. Herod had an expiration date; Jesus doesn't. Even the tomb couldn't hold Him. He remains alive and superior. Jesus reigns forever while Herod came to an end.

Worship is a response of reverence. One cannot truly worship without a reverential respect for the one being worshiped. In worshiping Jesus Christ, the worshiper is overcome with the awareness that he or she is approaching almighty God. When worship is true worship, one submits one's whole being to the moment.

The wise men expressed that kind of worship. When they encountered the Christ child, they knew the baby Jesus was the object of their search that had brought them quite a distance. The special star had caught and maintained their attention, Herod had given them specific guidance, and now the end of their quest was about to be realized. God's providence had directed the wise men all the way, and they had the faith and courage to go the distance. In the end, they exchanged their earthly treasures for heavenly treasure. Their example was opposite the shallow display of so much superficial worship.

The wise men were anxious to complete their journey. Jerusalem had not been a dead end. Insight was gained, and direction was given. In fact, it seems they were on their way that very night. They were more at home traveling by the night lights than by the sunlight. Besides, it was much cooler.

Suddenly, there was the star. The appearance served as a sign of confirmation as well as a guide. The star's reappearance surprised the wise men. Matthew dramatized the appearance by placing a "behold" at the moment. Maybe they were beginning to question their initial experience, but the star—the same one they initially saw—gave fresh energy to their long search.

This star was no ordinary star. Natural stars do not move as this star moved. It appeared; moved in a certain direction to lead them; and finally stood still (Matt. 2:9). Perhaps the star was an angel similar to the light the shepherds saw (Luke 2:9). Whatever its true nature was, the star served the purpose of guiding the first Gentiles who were doing their best to get to Christ. Heavenly help is always needed to find Jesus. God sent the magi exactly what was needed to complete their search successfully. Assurance, confirmation, and guidance were much-needed helps for the Christ-seekers.

When the wise men saw the star, they not only saw with their physical eyes, but they also saw with their hearts. The joy described is a joy that exceeded normal bounds. It was an overjoyed beyond measure joy (Matt. 2:10). This finder's joy has the look and feel of the joy of the plower who discovered treasure in the field (Matt. 13:24) and the merchant who recognized the pearl of great price (Matt. 13:45). The wise men had stepped into their moment by faith and discovered the explosive joy that comes from following God's direction.

The wise men entered the house—the place of worship. The nativity scene and the shepherds had come and gone. Joseph and Mary had taken up residence in a house. The house was probably middle class at best—certainly not that of the rich and famous. Those upper-class wise men, who were more accustomed to palatial mansions, went into a small, plain house where they finally met the one they had traveled so far to worship. In this situation, the carpenter's house became the place where the Master Carpenter was recognized.

The Christ child was with Mary, His mother. When they saw the child, the wise men saw with the eyes of faith and experienced what others had disregarded. The focus of their worship was clearly Jesus. They prostrated themselves in facedown worship before Him. It was an awesome, God-filled moment of soul worship—the kind that penetrates to the core of one's being.

The wise men not only paid homage, but they also opened their treasures. The gifts were gold, frankincense, and myrrh, gifts befitting royalty. Such gifts were proper adoration for a king. What they gave was an overflow of their hearts' worship. They were cheerful givers in the true sense of Christian giving (2 Cor. 9:7). They had found Jesus, and He had given them a breathtaking adventure. Honoring the newborn King became the experience of encountering the God of the universe.

God's guiding hand did not abandon the wise men after they found Jesus. They still faced an obligation to return to the wicked king. Herod already had a plan in place to eliminate the Christ child. Without God's directive to the wise men through a dream, one shudders to think what would have happened.

A dream revelation came to the wise men in the form of a warning. The details of the death plot were not revealed—only a no to going back to Herod. They didn't know the details, but they obeyed what they knew. So the wise men took another route back to their own country. It is significant that the wise men chartered a new course based on God's guidance. Perhaps they never knew how much their obedience to God's direction in their dream affected the lives of so many.

Herod, on his part, carried out his death scheme. He didn't handle being outwitted very well. His "thug side" surfaced again, and he ordered the killing of the babies in Bethlehem up to two years old. The Christ child escaped to Egypt, but the mothers of Bethlehem went through a mother's worst nightmare (Matt. 2:16–17)

Death had entered the Christmas story. As much as we would like to take it out, death slithered in through evil Herod's action of slaughtering innocent babies. While Jesus escaped this scheme, He would eventually fall victim to the scheme of the religious leaders. However, God prepared for and used even Jesus' death to fulfill the purposes of salvation. His power is such that He can take the worst of life and bring about God's good (Rom. 8:28). Christmas celebrates the birth of our Savior even in the midst of the suffering circumstances created by evil Herods.

The wise men demonstrated Abraham's faith by drawing their clues from the stars (Gen. 15:5–6). The Christ child followed a Moses pattern of escaping slaughter by child-killing soldiers. Bethlehem, the birthplace of the forgiven David, became the birthplace of the Promised One. Old Testament characters who have received godly promises found connecting points in this Christmas story. Matthew was quick to see the imprint and passed it to his readers. The Christmas story is the new happening of God, but it comes as a response to old promises. This new movement of God fulfilled promises made to those driven out of Eden. The way to God is still guarded but is available by grace through faith in Jesus Christ. Gentiles enter the Christmas story worshiping the Christ who will bruise the head of the evil one.

The wise men present a picture of what it means to worship Jesus. They stayed the course to bow down before the Lord. Here is commitment that pushes past the quitting points. This is an example of ones who put all on the altar without holding back. It is a commitment that worships in spite of the apathy of religious types or the hypocrisy of church Herods. Treasures are given because treasure is received. Such worship sustains Christians in this life until it is fully realized before the heavenly throne. So let us commit to the priority of worship, even after Christmas, and make the Savior first in our lives.

A design engineer of a major auto manufacturer was on vacation. He grew restless with inactivity and visited the local dealership. In the service department, the mechanics were puzzled over a car's breakdown. He walked up, looked at the car's motor, and told the amazed mechanics how to fix the problem. "Who are you?" asked the service department manager. The engineer replied, "I am the one who designed this car, and I know how to fix it."

Such is the story behind Christmas. The Designer of humankind has come to the world with His fixing solution. The Savior is born who will die on the cross and save us all from our sin. At Christmas and after Christmas, we worship the designer of this universe and His coming to this world to fix our sin and death problem. His salvation is available to all races, genders, and national origins. Wise men and women continue to seek the Savior.

Thanks be to God for His indescribable gift (2 Cor. 9:15). It started in the garden, arrived in Bethlehem, and continues today. Hallelujah, what a Savior!